# SF-Consensus

Poems of Park Je-chun

# Modern Poetry from Korea Series
## Published by Homa & Sekey Books

# SF-Consensus

## Poems of Park Je-chun

Translated by Chang Soo Ko

Homa & Sekey Books
Paramus, New Jersey

FIRST EDITION

Copyright © 2017 by Park Je-chun
English Translation Copyright © 2017 by Chang Soo Ko

This publication was supported by a grant from the Literature Translation Institute of Korea.

Library of Congress Cataloging-in-Publication Data

Names: Pak, Che-ch'ŏn, author. | Ko, Ch'ang-su, translator.
Title: SF-Consensus : poems of Park Je-chun / translated by Chang Soo Ko.
Description: First edition. | Paramus, New Jersey : Homa & Sekey Books, 2017.
Identifiers: LCCN 2016043829 | ISBN 9781622460304 (pbk.)
Classification: LCC PL992.62.C4175 A2 2017 | DDC 895.73/4--dc23
LC record available at https://lccn.loc.gov/2016043829

Published by Homa & Sekey Books
3rd Floor, North Tower
Mack-Cali Center III
140 E. Ridgewood Ave.
Paramus, NJ 07652

Tel: 201-261-8810, 800-870-HOMA
Fax: 201-261-8890
Email: info@homabooks.com
Website: www.homabooks.com

Printed in U.S.A.
1 3 5 7 9 10 8 6 4 2

# Table of Contents

CONTENTS

# Introduction

Park Je-chun was born in Seoul, Korea in 1945. He made his debut as a poet in 1966 through the monthly *Modern Literature*. He is one of the most important poets in Korea today. In 1984 he published *The Mind and Other Poems*, which included his poems translated into the English, French, Spanish, Chinese and Japanese languages. In 1997 the Cornell University press published a collection of English translations of his poetry as part of the Cornell East Asian Series. Park has published a total of 15 volumes of his poems. He has won the Modern Literature Prize, the Korea Poets Association Prize, the Woltan Literary Prize, the Gongcho Literary Prize and several other literary awards. He was invited to the 1984 International Writer's Program at Iowa University. Currently he is the representative of the Literature Academy in Seoul.

In reading Park's poetry one often gets the impression that he communicates intimately and intensely with nature and the transcendent realm as well as everyday human reality. His poetic prowess often creates esoteric yet gripping imagery, stories and episodes, demonstrating a transcendental spirit which ventures and journeys beyond the temporal. In his poetic work, one finds similarities to magic realist literature.

Whatever he imagines and conceives poetically he seems able to embody or evoke in vigorous Korean imagery, sounds and emotions. His poetry is largely marked by far-reaching poetic and metaphysical imagination and contemplation. Also, one can easily perceive how deeply he is involved with and immersed and steeped in poetry-writing. Widely read in world literature, with uncommon knowledge and understanding of East-Asian and Korean classics including Korean Buddhist, Confucian and Taoist literature and philosophy, Park writes, one might say, in the best tradition of poetic composition. He also uses the Korean language with remarkable plasticity and suppleness. He is a superb craftsman of Korean poetic diction, and his poetry as a whole shows an extraordinary esthetic sensibility and intuition.

As a long-time reader and translator of Park's poetry-- with a large bulk of powerful poetry yet to be translated and introduced to English-language readers, among others-- I feel increasingly fascinated about the ever-evolving world of his poetry.

Chang Soo Ko
September, 2016

# SF-Consensus

Poems of Park Je-chun

## 1. Ring's House

A round trace like a moon-halo surrounded
The third finger from which I removed the ring after 33
 years.
I'll never wear a ring again, I told myself.

As I looked up at the skies in the middle of night,
There that ring was floating.
A ring which might accommodate me like a belt
When I thrust my body into it--
And not a mere finger--
Gazed down at me with gloating eyes.

"As namelessness opens sky and earth,
Naming is mother of everything."
I seemed to hear someone whisper like aging Lao-tze.

So, it's the ring that's been etched on the body and mind.

Wearing another ring over the moonlight ring,
I relocated my residence to the ring's house.

## 2. The Spruce's House

I went to see the spruce which he planted and
Under which he was subsequently buried when he died.
I saw a name
Which has dimmed in the tree's breast,
Which my hand can no longer touch.

I read his words written in each leaf of the spruce.
His words which soared from the roots of the spruce were
    drenched with sap.
I could read with my eyes and feel with my hands
The letters of dewdrops forming over his eyes.

His soul seeping into the roots of the spruce
Past the trunk and the branch
Was an autobiography
Soaring into the sky riding on the welcoming sunbeams
Gleaming in each leaf.
A life of love, parting, joy and sorrow,
Riding on the fan's wind rising from each branch and leaf
Like some aurora,
Was wafting like the sun's halo
Over the treetop of the spruce.

The name inscribed in the breast of the spruce
Hugging its dark brown body
Which had become one with the tree--
I thought someday somebody would read
My tree's words too.

## 3. SF-UFO

Some stones live turning their backs to their peers;
In the Jaunri valley such queer chaps are numerous.
Some of them drip with sweat and face the wall,
In meditation posture.
Their body riddled with holes--
Some sport with all kinds of fancies
Together with water traveling through the holes;
Others dream of becoming water while practicing full-body
    prostrations.
Amidst them all I often speak to a UFO--
A name I gave to the flat quartz rock
Which looked like a discus.
As a legendary snake grows into a dragon in a thousand
    years,
I trust someday it will soar over the Jaunri valley and be-
    come a star.
It will not budge even if I kick it.
When I, all naked, mount the UFO and lie on my back,
I receive the ceaseless Morse codes it sends
Though I cannot decode them.
I cannot dismiss the thought
That at one time there was someone
Who gave me the name of UFO.

## 4. Peregrine Bird

Daubed with a bowlful of red dyestuff,
My eyes dream of the quartz at the foot of Baeknokdam
    lake.
Daubed with a can of blue dyestuff,
My mind clings to the dead tree
At the fringe of Heavenly Lake.

Winds! Let this tattered dream flutter.
Winds! Pray inscribe your pain
Over this hardened mind.

The longing aroused by living in this world has doubled,
Now drifting through the nearby heavens.
The joy of dying in this world has become a bird,
Now flying through the remote skies.
The star's blood blending into wine,
The rainbow's flesh washed out with wine.
Now,
Abandoning everything...

Where in the earth,
Which branch of the heavenly path?

Discarding all...
The anger that glares, having become oak charcoal;
The grief that resounds the vacant paulownia tree;
The sorrow of the black alder, devoid of trunk or branch,
That has become a guardian pole.

The thunderclaps and lightning flashes that devour even the
    lightning flames;
The Indian ink island that has risen high solitarily,
Having shattered its bones.

Let us go--
Outside the world that moves as a mere lowly creature,
Outside the painting that wriggles alive as a drop of water.
Let us leave swiftly for some island.

## 5. The Valley-God's Face

The eyebrows are far apart. The bald head has a protruding brow. The nose-line is sunk as low as the lowest ridge-line.

That's the valley-god's face drawn by artist O Su-Hwan. But then O Su-Hwan has never met the valley-god. All the same, he persistently draws the valley-god. After he and I booze it up, the valley-god multiplies. If so, who can be the model of the valley god O Su-Hwan creates? Deciding to get the model fee tonight, I closely examine the catalogue for possible evidence. But I can find no painting entitled "The Valley-God's Face." Whose face is the valley-god's face I saw? By chance looking into the mirror, I find the valley-god smirking there. Ghosts are different indeed! For material evidence I take a picture of it. Developing the negative, I find nothing imprinted there!

My conclusion is that the valley-god has no face.
But then has O Su-Hwan portrayed nothingness?
Nihil!
How hard he has painted nothingness!

Note: The valley-god: from "Tao Te Ching" by Lao-tze.

## 6. SF-Consensus

I see you stretching yourself as golden flower stamen
Inside the petals of the bellflower.
Having received chi (qi) treatment,
For the first time after birth I look into my navel.
I feel the cosmic waves
Spreading from navel to navel inside the petals of the bell-
    flower--
I see you stretching yourself as golden flower stamen,
Having accepted all the dazzling sunbeams and the glaring
    snowflakes,
Brimful in the petals, in the navels.
They say my life heated by building fire fully in the abdo-
    men
And the chronic coughing fits of Mother and her mother
Were all inherited from there.
When I thrust my hand inside the flower petals,
Suddenly the skies of the outer world pile up
As thirty three heavens, level upon level;
There I find Mother's navel
Blooming as a bellflower in one of the heavens.
I see from here where I stand
The path leading into the flowers of Creation;
There I sense the hand firmly pressing my navel.

## 7. Sky Reading Glasses: First Essay on Poetics

One day as I looked through my reading glasses
I learned that many things already had on reading glasses.

Even the moonbeams of the skies were wearing reading
glasses, peering into the four corners of our life.

The king mantis and king ants of the grass field,
Wearing reading glasses, were ferreting out details from
within the grasses and the earth.

Going out to Yangsuri in springtime,
I found the fancy-free river and the fish
And the sunbeams resting on their scales,
Even those grains of sand holding their breath on the sea-
bed,
Were all wearing reading glasses,
Watching smilingly the lowly things that aimed to harm
them.

Thereafter,
I decided to wear reading glasses when I met people,
Pretending not to notice their stench or their avarice
As when I want to make friends with the hills and the rivers.

## 8. Inn

What could I ever know? I depart as the ticket directs. A broken cloud comes along. Beneath the snow filling the sunny southern garden, there lurks a solidly empty darkness. It's dead or alive, here and there, like the idle wind. In time will appear a place where I must land.

## 9. The Words of an Oak

A bell sounds from the sky.
As I look up
Fruit hang in each branch of the sky-high oak tree.
They seem to waft apart from the branches.
At times I cannot hear the bell.
They have stayed there all along since last autumn.
Though the winter flows and the spring flows,
They don't seem to think of approaching the earth.
Blinking dark eyes among the deep green new leaves
They pay no attention to snow, rain, or wind.
Though bitten by ants that visit from the earth,
They don't budge.

As I listen,
I hear bell sounds.
The bell sounds carry some meaning.
Since I have not unraveled the mind's affairs,
I cannot decode the meaning.
Sometimes the bell sounds loud.
Perhaps they converse among themselves.
Carrying all over their body bunches of fruit hardened by
    life,

They must search for a way to communicate with one man
on earth.

The bell sounds approach.

They tell me to make bell sounds.

They tell me to become some tree

And abandon man's words.

The bell sound, the bell sound, the bell sound.

## 10. Hell's House

I build a house among the leaves; bored, I build a house in
the stone.
Being exhausted, I build a house in the water.

I build a house in the wind, or in the rain, or in the smoke.
In the end, I build a house even in the calendar time such as
August 1990.

In the house I build there is no window, no wall, no roof;
no floor trodden by anyone entering or anyone leaving,
or doors to be opened. Suddenly one could crush it and
then rebuild it. One could build it somewhere near
Neptune if tired of the earth.

The snail carries on its back its own house but retreats into
it for rest. A house lighter and stronger than the sea-
shell's house which closes when someone peers. A
transparent house not noticed by anyone's eyes, a house
that stays clean for some fifty years without being wall-
papered or painted.

Yet my eyes can see. My eyes can see in one glance my own
house with smoked traces here and there, old spider

webs, decaying smell, shameful scarlet flesh sprouting in scars, and sinful affection.

## 11. Drinking Tea

I accept you into my inside.
Your breaths, your eye-beams, your fragrance
Fill my inside to the full.
The sun's elements mix with white blood,
Pluto's spirit mixes with red blood.
I turn into mine your career that's ending, having become a
    star of the Milky Way.

I accept you deep into my inside.
I hear the darkness underneath the earth, and
The cold and the pain I experience awake all alone,
Which are carried along the thin line of the nerve.
All alone I fumble, crawl, run and collapse
And feel the crouching time of silence hugging the broken
    knee.

I slowly forget you in my inside, you slowly forget me in
    your inside.
Surrounded by hot breaths, fragrant eyebeams and soft air,
I raise one by one
The things that were discarded in my past life, that were
    scattered and now roll about.

I cleanse with the water of gleaming sleep
The pain seeping my flesh and soul.

Drinking a cup of tea,
At times watching a sleeping star.

## 12. The Bird's Hat

The hills I've visited are wearing hats.
Some hills wear rock hats, some wear tree hats.
Mont Blanc was sporting a snow hat;
Mount Baekdu, which I have not yet visited,
Wears a water hat, they say.

I go around wearing a bird hat,
Though more homely than the feather hat
The Kokuryo men wore.
It must be an expression of the mind to mean
It wants to fly in the skies.
As Changjie made letters imitating bird footprints,
Someday I'll use the bird's frame as a model
To be reborn.

This morning
Watching the peaks of Mount Dobong
Gleaming in the distance with a rock hat,
I think my body is like a mountain
Though I wear a bird hat.

The trees that set down their roots inside me
So that they may not be able to fly around,

The bulky rocks pressing down on their liver
So that they may not grow any longer…
So that the tigers, foxes, wolves living in each cave
May breathe and live freely,
I think my body too has become a hill.

## 13. The Annual Rings of the Oriental Oak

The annual rings just carved out of the oriental oak
Glimmer pink like a baby's skin.
As I listen intently,
A baby twig's cries sliced by a saw blade emanate loudly.
The sunbeams, winds, water-drops that lived together
In the mountain
Were locked instantly in the paths of the annual rings.
As I step into that path
Grasshoppers rise startled,
Raising their front legs ready for combat;
A king ant wielding its head the size of a lantern
Thrusts its feelers towards me like lances.
It's not me, it's not me.
As I fumble my way, drenched in the oriental oak's tears,
Dark stains gather in the midst
Like the sun's black spot.
In there the oriental oak's soul greets me
In a meditation posture.
Who are you?
I could not respond till the end.

## 14. Imagination Play

Those which exist in this world--each and everyone--
Ceaselessly leave over their body as poetry
The wounds they experience all alone,
Not to mention meetings and partings.

Though I've omitted out of indolence some of them like
The eyebeams of twilight, the shudders of white snow,
For fifty years I've transcribed their poems into letters.

When I yell sounds that do not come out as sound all alone
Their shrieks whip up like a rod the blood vessels within me,
Squeeze up the bowels within me,
And pound like a sandbag the flesh within my body.
I too write a poem in my body.

Though they claim it is poetry, these records
Become poetry or rubbish
Depending on who reads them.

Tonight,
I indulge a sad but ecstatic fancy
Imagining that you make this scribble into a poem.

## 15. Rain's House

Perhaps--that was the forest of nut pines.

Rain--a soft green rain fell on the nut pine.

No--it seemed the nut pine could fall over the rain.

Yes--it seemed to gently clean the nut pine's body.

Perhaps--my hand scrubbing my sick wife's back was like that.

Pressure--I could not possibly put pressure...

Simply--the rain fell on the nut pine as if hugging it lightly.

So--the peace seeped in so gracefully.

Perhaps--the nut pine was sick in some part.

Suddenly--my sick wife, no longer by my side,

Alone--seemed to be standing in the rain as the nut pine.

Now--I too getting wet with rain

Just so--was leaning on the nut pine shivering feebly.

## 16. Water's House

From a vacant room a bird murmurs and hums.
When I look in, only a faint fragrance
Radiates from a white porcelain kettle,
The bird's chirping to be found nowhere.
While boiling the sparrow's-tongue tea,
Did the leaves resembling the sparrow's lips
Have friendly talk?
As I look absent-mindedly inside the kettle,
I seem to notice a glimpse of some sound pattern in the
    water.
The sunlight overflowing the treetop
And the darkness inside the earth that the roots tensely
    sucked up
Mixed one with another.
They are giving or receiving water patterns
Featuring the sounds the water wants to make
And the sounds the leaf wants to make.
We must wipe out the darkness in man's body.
We must encircle the whole body with a clean spirit.
When I listen to the sounds,
They taste so delicious, so sweet.
This ecstasy of filling the glass to the full

With those delicious sounds poured from the white-
porcelain kettle.

Today I ate to satiety the clear leaf's words resembling bird
sounds,

And the water's words neither audible nor visible.

## 17. Every Day a Good Day

On a day when somebody gently evokes my thought
I look for a pine grove.

I entrust my body to pine needles
Which only by a glimpse break through a block.

Where the mind's place is torn, they call sunbeams
Stitching the torn places stitch by stitch with sunlight nee-
    dles.

I sit in the pine grove the whole day.
In the end I become a pine flower, sending away softly on
    the wind
All yellow-ripe cares.

I send them away flying, hoping
The vacant-sky god will take them.

## 18. Untitled: Cow-Seeking Painting

If flower blooms
If flower fades

Even if wind blows
Even if wind ceases

Being pelted by rain
Taking shelter from rain

Writing poetry
Abandoning poetry

I'm writing a poem entitled "Untitled."
I'm writing a poem whose end only you and I can predict.

## 19. What I See When I Close My Eyes
--Imitating Ma-tsu


There cannot be anything I can see when I close my eyes.

It's a chimera that I can see with the mind's eyes.

I give you a brick;

Try and rub it into a mirror.

What part of you would the mirror reflect?

When you don't know whether your eyes are open or closed,

Then and only then you'll see yourself.

You are

A drop of dew that rolls over a tree's leaf this morning,

A cock's crow that bursts out of the dew.

By abandoning you

The laughter of those alive in this world

Will only bloom to the full.

## 20. Matiere

The pictures of trees I've drawn are beyond count;
There's only one canvas.
Whenever I want to see all kinds of trees I've drawn,
I raise the knife
And scratch the pictures of trees off the canvas coat after
coat.
The faces of trees that appear on the canvas
Are always plain faces.
In order to seek the face of the tree hiding behind the face
I have to erase the bare face.
When I lift the color painted on the tree's face
Another color of the sap awaits me.
The tree's face that emerges when I erase
The naked face of the tree is not the face of any tree;
So I paint a new face again.
I put the natural faces on a tree carrying stars on the top,
A tree that bears wings on each branch,
A tree on each of whose leaves beetles and ladybugs are
drawn;
I paste colors on the canvas and
Scratch out colors again, looking for the face of the only
tree.

For the face of the one tree that has embraced all colors,
For an autobiography of the tree's face
I put face upon face, attach face to face,
And detach face from face.

## 21. Moonlight Mirror

An operation the more curious and mysterious
The more I think…
An operation of drawing stone out of fragrance,
And drawing fragrance out of stone.

As if it were the moon's halo
That blooms apace out of the granite;
As if it were the clusters of flower by the river
That emerge out of the dark in the middle of night.

Peeping into the moonlight mirror
That is soft even if it's stone,
That hides a stone in itself though it's fragrant.

I want to take myself out of you
Plucking you with a chisel,
Trimming you with a chisel.
Each night
I eat up the moonlight mouthful after mouthful.
I drill into you till you turn into a ring.

I dig into my inside that has become the moon.

## 22. Snowy Day – Love Story

Let's go out to the field on a snowy day.
Let's read the letters God sends us.
The trees that fly their long hair like a pretty woman
Become vowels.
And stones become consonants.
The punctuation marks
Of the snowmen who stand here and there;
The exclamation marks of the insects
That run about in the snow field;
Amidst the remote blizzard's kisses that approach as ellipsis
God's love letters fill the whole field.

Let's go out to the field on snowy days.
Warming up our frozen cheeks
In the ice-sheet mirror frozen utterly under the snow field--
Matilda,
Let us, you and I, read the story of love
That has not been fulfilled.

## 23. Transparent Fairy

On God's white paper where the blizzard whirls
Somebody pastes a lot of transparent dyes
With a transparent brush.

Are you aware of
The sky and sea that suddenly leap out of the green
Each time the brush passes by;
Trees and flowers that jump out of the spectrum of colors;
That nature's breaths--the nature's respiratory organ--
From which eyes, ears and wings soar.
When the transparent fairies of March the month of my
    birth
Roam in the water, flower trees and the winds,
Everybody's heart swells up.
Not only the frog and ladybug
But the quartz stones cleaning their body in the water---
Their haunches become tight.

What's most exciting is to become
A flower tree and wait.
Haze is blown out with each breath;
The sunlight's eyes, the sunlight's lips sprout
When the transparent fairies leap around within me.

It is to look for you and meet you again
In that nature's life.

## 24. Ginger Plant Game

Getting up in the middle of night,
I eat the stars and the moon,
Melting and rolling on the tongue's tip the light that fills the
whole mouth,
Refraining from saying whose crying it is.

Sweeping the sky piece by piece with the well-ground cres-
cent-moon sickle blade
Searching in this night the Milky Way of this star and that
star where I was born.
Like cutting into small pieces the darkness which fills the
mouth.

The goat sucker's moaning voice drilling annual rings into
the tree,
The sounds of frogs jumping about in the middle of night
Twinkling as the Milky Way...
At last I open the leaves and the sprouts within me.

Going around the whole Milky Way in the middle of night
Shedding sweat again and again
The Huayen desolation finds the body of the ginger plant at
early dawn.

We cannot say we've seen it--
The Huayen silence embraces the body as it is.

## 25. The Day I Went to See the Magic Lily

I went to see the magic lily, but

I saw my love's pigtail ribbon flaming like a coral.

That ribbon's flame shifted on to the fire within me

Which I thought had gone out long ago.

The flame did not go out

Though I poured a bottle of wine

To put out the flame that started again.

The flame that spread out to the magic lily field,

My love's eyebeams that stuck into the magic lily petals as
stamen

While I watched the magic lily flames that were poignantly
beautiful

I became dead drunk, my eyesight ever dimming.

Finally I became

A flame that burned gradually into the magic lily stamen.

## 26. Ecstatic Game

Like God, like Buddha

An ecstatic play
By which I cleanse and release one by one
The dirty, puss-filled and wounded stars
Within me.

Dandelions and asters wash out their stains in the sun-
beams;
Even dogs and cats
Lick up their own wounds.

The ecstatic game by which
I straighten, tie up and raise one by one
The stars within me that have twisted, stuck together and
distended loosely.

Thank you really for teaching me the nature's method
To clean out with the tongue and wash out with sunbeams
Even the darkness--dazzlingly, dazzlingly.
Still, alone, dark--
I'll convey them to whoever may come my way.

## 27. Four Quartets Game

I send clouds floating
On the day I want to see somebody.
Letting lotus flowers blooming all over the mirror lake,
Tuning in to FM 5 channel and listening to the requiem,
I hug somebody's flaming shirt and get a burn.

I'm always naked in those moments.
I take off the flaming shirt in advance.
For I don't want to witness somebody who,
Hugging me and jumping around burnt by fire,
Jumps into the lotus pond and
Pastes the clay at the bottom layer upon layer onto his burnt
     places.
For I don't want to get blind by
The fragrance of the lotus that has put down
Its roots into the clay at the bottom
Or the bleakness of the lotus.

For my intestines,
My memories
Have already been burnt and have shrunk
Though I don't wear flaming shirts.

Dunking the whole body into the mirror-lake
In time with the melodies of the requiem wandering about
Among the cotton clouds.
I go down to the bottom and resurface.
That day I go out in search of somebody who is wearing a
  flaming shirt.
The scar from the burn I'll get from her again--
I want to etch it into my body like a decoration.

## 28. Wanderings

Do you know the sea that prostrates like a fish
In the remote darkness in the north?
Do you know the spawn of eggs that have not yet hatched?
Do you know what will be born out of those eggs?
Do you know the egg that will eventually emerge as a bird?

The moments of time we prostrated in the depths of the
    sea as chunks of ice
The moments of time we kept silent in the darkness of that
    sea as balls of fire
The moments of time we held our breath waiting for the
    beloved woman's egg

You must know
Earlier in life each of us was an egg, too;
You must remember
Mother's sea, Mother's darkness.
You must recall
That morning we played the pipe made from the lion's
    bones.
You must recall
That night we flew in the sky riding on the phoenix.

Again, becoming an egg again
Becoming that sea, that fish,
That darkness, that fire, that water
Becoming a joy of meeting another world beyond the one
     world
Like somebody who carried his own tomb in his bosom
Like somebody who had put into his pocket a whale
That would fly away somewhere
Like someone who has returned to their own place
Their world's sky and land

Do you know the dream that lives the dream
Like the dream within the dream.

## 29. With the Bird

When I look at a new leaf sprouting on a tree,
I feel it's like a little bird.
When I keep an eye on the second-hand numbers
Which the tree's branches show tangling together
As if it were the face of a pocket watch.
They take a posture to leave the tree any moment and fly
    towards the sky.
I too keep an eye on the face of that tree.
Perhaps the numbers will hide into the textures
As the tree grows
And finally remain as the pattern on the plank cut off.
Even then somebody will announce the time to fly away like
    birds.
I think that the things that sprout like leaves and snow
From the clay's roots
Always dream of such flights
From the very beginning.

## 30. Green Moss Dress

One day I'll rear a flower
That puts forth buds
By letting down lotus roots
Among the straws, nails and sands, all mingled,
In the clay of the breast.

One day I'll shed my mind
That sheds its skin and the flaming flesh
In the time of the desert,
By borrowing the body of a parrot
And spreading wings of red twilight
In the remote, remote western sky.

Caressing the green moss dress that puts down roots
Putting ears to the warm lungs of the rocks and ivy dresses
Deeply breathing in their bright breaths and fragrance
One day I'll make tranquilizer pills
By maturing and ripening the indignation I experience
Living as a human being.

## 31. Time Travel

Before I saw the immortals sleeping in Tomb No. 4 of the
  Tonggu Five Tombs
I didn't believe the immortals
Floating airily in the sky.
Before I met the sun's god, the moon's god,
And my father's black-smith god who was with them.
Before Father suddenly looked back at me
And smiled like cotton
I didn't believe my father's life in the nether world.
Before he took out a clump of iron
Out of the water where he had been tempering it,
Before the thunder that burst out of the iron darker than
  night
Crushed my fifty years in this world,
I didn't believe that my life would not end here.
Before I noticed another sky in that tomb
Before I saw the remote place towards which
The immortals were flying,
Straddling the dragon and the phoenix.

I didn't know who I was.
I didn't realize my identity
Even after I had made that time travel.

## 32. Foxglove Flower

When I put my hands in the clay, somebody emerged grasp-
ing my hands.
When I parted the earth wanting to see the warmth,
Bodiless thin roots were caught by the fingers.
They may be the foxglove roots that were swinging quite
drunk
With their stems burdened with Canterbury bells
Which could not utter any voice through the summer.
When I dried the foxglove in the wind, it was the dried fox-
glove.
When steamed in wine, they called it the steamed foxglove.
Since my blood has become cold with my aching back feel-
ing chilly,
I might lay the mat here to lie down for warmth.
I might bloom as foxglove flower on some June day,
And cool in the wind my blushing face as well as my warm
breast
With the longings for another world simply
Hidden among the roots.

## 33. Where the Sun

I placed the go-game board in the water.
I used white and black quartz stones as go pieces
Whose corners and sides had been rounded and worn
By a-hundred-year–old currents.

The go-game one plays alone--
Where shall I lead
The weary hobbyhorse
That I've driven here and there,
Having shoved my youth's dreams into a dead end.
I couldn't avert my eye
Even when the moonlight tipped the bait.

Covering the remaining life shivering over the go-board
With the blue mosquito net,
Offering my flesh that smells of burning to the mosquitos
    all night.

I was plodding through the desert's time
Beyond that sand field
Shedding sweat deep in the water.

Until in the go-board's darkness
A red quartz stone rose like the sun.

## 34. My Star

I look up at the sky looking for a star that exists there
But is invisible.
I fumble inch by inch each of the skies
Divided into 365 different parts,
Looking for my star whose eyes alone remain, roaming,
As well as the face that is invisible but drifts there.
Each day I pursue only the shadows
That disappear by glimpses into the next sky,
Having become a red crab, a black beetle and a blue longi-
corn.

Though at times a rainbow spreads
Or a lightning flashes over a distant mountain,
I've never thought of following them.
Only my heart leaps because I feel my star is there all the
time.
And I fall asleep hoping to meet her there someday.

## 35. Chuang-tze Costume Play

As suddenly I looked into the mirror while reading Chuang-
tze's "Wanderings,"
I was not there, but my deceased wife was alive, reading a
book.
I wondered what book--she was reading "On Arranging
Things."
On the wall there was a quilt with the picture of a butterfly.

As I looked more closely, in one corner of the mirror,
The Chuang-tze's roc the size of a sparrow was flying
through the sky.
It was flying toward the Southern Ocean still carrying me.

That's so—so far I've been teaching
The fools in that dream how to live;
That way I live while being dead.

When I peered into the Great Happiness,
I recalled that I had died getting consoled by all things,
Having heaven and earth as my coffin
And the sun, moon and stars as my burial accessories.

Being on the earth a fodder for the crows and black kites

Being in the earth fodder for insects and ants…
I'm still going on surveying the vast ocean,
Snatching somebody's food.

Suddenly I look into the mirror, and my wife disappears;
I'm still pruning "Wanderings."
A quilt with the picture of a ship on the wall.
Beatitude, indeed! I'm still shuttling between dream and life.

## 36. Roaming Heaven and Earth

So be it.
Even on such a busy day
It'll be still better for me
To ride the whirl wind in a moment, climbing up to the sky
     within me,
Sprawling on the cloud, and visiting the Southern Ocean.

Hey, buddies, do you have no vacation?
I talked with me that lives within me over Kakao Talk.
He sends me an emoticon that smirks, saying:
Why so hurry, you'll get an eternal vacation when you die.

The Chuang-tze's roc within me murmurs:
In that country when you want to rest
You'd just take out batteries temporarily like a robot.

Huainanzi says: Blessings and Curses in Disguise.
For it'll be a blessed life
To live a busy life in this country.

## 37. Mind-Reading Method

A wine glass speaks to me.
By this time, the wine in the glass,
Fried kelp brought as snack,
The chair upholding my haunches,
Even the arms that prop the chin
All alike speak to me.

All this is the joy of living alone.
Having only obeyed the moonlight and starlight,
I too speak with my eyebeams.

Today's subject is
The aurora of the emperor star near the Big Dipper
Which my eyebeams and moonbeams,
Eyebeams and starlight meet and produce on such occasions.

I drink a toast to the fate of that aurora.
But this time the extraterrestrial alien may appear.
It's quite a sight.

The night sky, the star, the moon read my mind.
I too read their minds.

The mind can be easily read if only one looks.

I readily surrender the moonlight, starlight and eyebeams;
In this night, the color of wine becomes the moon and the
stars.

## 38. Living Alone

After I left him behind in the stone house
I too began to cut the water plants.

In the face of the mind's cliff
Beyond which I could not advance
The projecting rocks of longing, repentance, and solitude
Served as support columns

Calling the halo clouds for the roof,
Each time I treated the heat with rainstorm clouds.

A handsome house--
Sitting on the pavilion, I cooled my breast
With ice from the remote skyway.

Don't come near.
Producing toxic air, soaring like cloud all alone,
I enclosed myself in a thorn hedge.
I didn't want to hurt anybody any longer.

## 39. Very Pretty Tree

I saw a very pretty tree.
I saw a very pretty woman
As water runs and flower blooms
When long hair sways in the tree like wind.

I wanted to sit in the stone for millennia.
I wanted to call out the woman hiding in there
When water runs and flower blooms.

As I'd dig out the woman from within me,
I wanted to call out the angel from within the tree.

Matilda, who became a tree
Playing with the tree all day long like that--
Pray let your roots down into me that has become stone.

## 40. Lighting the Lamp

The path of a bird that flies up to the sky now
The path of the sap in the twig where now a flower-bud
    opens
Deep in the spring where water rises now
The grass roots in the earth which the wind shakes now.

I offer up to you, Matilda,
The dazzling light of this lamp
Granted to me for all those unions.

The wailing of the rain that coils into every grass stem
The pain in every grain of sand that flows down now
The blue dusk's twilight sorrow
That forms the gorges for each shaking hill
The darkness that remains a sinew
In every bone of the things that are alive now.

I light the lamp and
Offer up the lamp for all partings.

## 41. Bird

The birds I send away on their wings
Are not the birds of nature.
I don't know what name to give to that bird that,
Sky-high, beyond the stars that float there,
Flies to another sky—
I don't know what name to give to that bird.
Carrying several wings, tongues and brains
Over the wing and head;
Pray wander around to every nook and cranny of this mind
Faster than light, farther than darkness.
Bird, you have flown away
As this finger pointed without any possible meaning,
As this glance directed.
Today I should become a bird suddenly
And fly away with full speed.
Pray stay floating as stars in another sky
Past the stars that float there high in the sky.
Your voice that wails with the whole body
Gets higher or lower,
Being starlight that each time
Becomes bright or dim.

## 42. The Day I Buddy up with the Black Swan

A paint brush composes a sentence over the winter sky
With a sweeping stroke.
That sentence in seal-style characters--
Letters may be invisible, but
This joy of reading the sentence!

The brush daubs ice-dye amply--
Ice eyes twinkle
Though the face may be invisible.
This joy of just listening
While the eyeball writes and reads.

Is it because I live alone
With no anger, regret or solitude?
When that letter looks like a letter meaning dumb,
I shut my mouth;
When that letter looks like a letter meaning laugh,
I burst out laughing.

That
Lone bird
That has emerged in the winter sky
To be friendly with me--

This joy of befriending that black swan!

Though there's no place for me to visit,
The joy of reading books together with bird-friends
If only I have that sky;
This one lifetime is worth living.

## 43. Thathata Play

When I first learned to play billiards
I saw people's heads as billiard balls.
When I was learning to play go, people's heads looked like
  go pieces.

When I looked into the mirror
After shaving my head,
My glittering head looked like a billiard ball or a go piece.
It's not that I want to learn something more;
Someone must be telling me I should learn more.
That's why I came to examine other people's heads;
Thus I saw them carrying over their buttocks or in their
  pockets
The heads that should have been found over their necks.
I met even people who bragged about keeping them in a
  safe to begin with.

But then I discovered that unlike man
Trees and flowers, rocks and hills, water and wind
Were living forgetful of the troublesome heads.
Like all things and phenomena of heavens and earths
They were just living like that in their own places.

Each time our eyes met,

All things and phenomena all alike told me to live just
thathata.

So I too decided to forget about my glittering head.

## 44. Firefly
--Poetics No. 11


When I first met the firefly,
Clutched it in my two hands and
Put my eyes close to the light,
The light of the jade pendant brightened inside my dark
　　eyes--
I want to convey that light to you.

When I first met the snow flake,
Upheld the snow flake in my two hands, and
Put my flaming brow to that light,
That jade eyebeam radiated coolly inside my head--
I want to convey that eyebeam to you.

One day I sobbed burying my face between my two knees,
I suddenly looked up at the night sky, and
Chestnut-sized stars in the dark looked down upon me
With burning eyebeams, burning up the agony
Boiling in my heart with diamond starlight--
I want to convey that starlight to you.

My friend,
Though our feet may misstep into life's mire,

Struggling without being able to get out of that mire,
We suddenly shake off stains and grime of this life,
Making headway unhindered from this hill to that,
From this sky to that with the power of the gut:
That eyebeam of our mothers--
I want to convey that eyebeam to you.

## 45. Before a Mummy

Shrunken like a bony goat, he lay there. His soul, which had
escaped out of his chalky chunks of flesh, had not re-
turned to him as yet. He's already no more than a hand-
ful of earth; someone still prevents clumps of his flesh
from decaying.

Error lies with one's self;
Standing in the sunlight, wind and rain
One should have shared pieces of one's flesh with birds
that visited
And let insects taste one's blood.
One should have let the disburdened soul
Depart to another world whistling tunes.

But, that's a notion on the part of someone foolish like me;
even now, before spectators who peer into him once,
feel curious, sneer or thoughtlessly pass by, he mumbles:

I'll return; In Africa or anywhere else, I'll find the place.
I'll ignore your life worth a hundred years.
With my eyes closed in dignity
I'll wait for the soul that'll finally come back.

## 46. Tiger's Wedding Day

In simple terms, the craft of jewelry involves
Striking, polishing, rubbing, scrubbing
To bring out shining gloss.
As if sesame oil has been applied,
It must become glossy and bright.
As if offering 100-day prayers or sacrifices,
You must caress and rub it with all your heart to produce
    soft gloss;
It must become lucid like a mirror that reflects a shimmer-
    ing face and
Like a windowpane you can see through clearly
To show in there the shining naked body.
You must let the twinkling eyes meet and
Embrace the pounding heart's breaths;
Only then for the first time it becomes your own.
After fox rain has fallen
Into the ears, dimples,
Breasts, buttocks, groins, knee-crooks, and
Protruding shady gaps, only then
Enchanting love consummates with overhanging rainbows.
And the tiger's wedding day will arrive.
Isn't it so, my love?

## 47. Straw-Hat Cinema

Do you know the straw-hat cinema?

A straw-hat striped with a fragmented 16mm movie film
    strip--
When you put on that straw-hat
The sunlight projector rolls smoothly charrr charrr;
A movie rolls away
Nonchalantly shoving aside my lifetime in my brain.

Two women for one man, two men for one woman,
Or else fantasy and solitude--
Life is fantastic or sad, tragedy or comedy, all alike.

Don't get born into the world,
It's painful to die.
Don't abandon the world, it's painful to be born anew.
More briefly, it's all painful to die or live.
I recall what Priest Wonhyo said.

My observation: it's futile to separate death from life.
You may replace the movie film when fancy hits you,
And enjoy whatever life you choose at will.

That straw-hat, 40 years later,

Today appears in my memory's monitor.

Starting today, I'll put on the straw-hat whenever I go to
bed.

## 48. Seaweed

What to do with this life like seaweed
That has melted into agar-agar.
Having written and read a few lines of words
I raise my eyes because of the slashing pain in the waist.
The day is declining already.
When I was young, days flowed slowly
And I was worried
Someone might take away all the sky's rainbows;
As I grew older
I failed to revive even the names of the birds
Who woke me from my dawn's sleep.
I turn my ears trying to attach meaning
To the night bird's wailing voices.
At first shoulders tightened,
The waist ached;
At times acute pain shoots through the waist and then the
    leg.
In such moments
I'd readily leave this place to go to
Zhongbei country which a man called Wu once visited
Which has no rain, wind, frost or dew
Or any grass, plants and trees, or beasts,
Disease, conflict, envy or boasting

Where people can live a hundred years quite naked
And die like dreaming.
But that will never happen.

Never happen.

## 49. Memory of Songs

That day I saw the ball-like sun disappear
Beyond the western hill, goaded by a song.

At dawn next day I played that disc once more.
The singing voice rose higher and higher,
Then the disc stopped, and the sun rose again.

My diary when I was 15 or 16 years old
Was riddled with lies like that.

It was in those days that
My whole body itched with shame
Each time I heard a song.

50 years I lived like that--
The diary of the 50 years of age
When truth written down changes into lies.

This night too I'm overwhelmed by a song
And meet the moon that rises over the hillock.

## 50. Green Moss Dress

One day I'll cultivate a flower that
Will bloom bud after bud
Having lowered lotus roots
Through straws, nails and sand grains all jumbled,
In the patch of clay in the breast-field.

One day, I'll borrow the body of
The diamond parrot, and shed boldly the burning flesh
In the desert's time and the mind sloughing its skin,
And spread scarlet twilight wings
In the faraway western sky.

Touching the green moss dress
That puts down its roots into the rocks,
Putting my ears over the warm hearts of the rocks and the
    moss dress,
Deeply breathing in the fragrance of their bright breathing
    sounds.

One day I'll rot and ferment fully the anger I experience
Living as a man, and make them into tranquilizer pills.

## 51. Dream within Dream

Among flowering plants there are ones that bloom
Only when their stems dry up.
--Is it an affair beyond Jordan river one crosses at death?
--Where would such river be?
--There are surprisingly so many flowers that bloom
in places neither light nor dark.

Placing that Jordan bird-flower in the vase--
I occasionally shuttle between life and death
Though I'm not sure whether they are the same or not.
--When time hangs idly on my hands,
The balls of the Jordan bird-flower, which costs a few hun-
     dred won a bunch, have yellow eyeballs resembling cat
     eyes with red rims. And they keep an eye on me.
--Time must hang idly on their hands too.

One day when rain has drenched even the air
Suddenly all flowers hang down their heads.
--Moisture is antipathetic to them.

Even the water that fills my human body and tumbles
Has moisture spreading out at times.

--In such moments they too will hang down their heads
again.


As I tell someone in dreams about the dreams I dream in
dream
I can't tell whether they are dreams or not.
--Am I the Jordan bird-flower?


Sorrow and longing, becoming an illness, hurt the body.
--In such nights even dreams get hurt and crack thinly.
Among men there are those who produce sariras at death
Only when they shake off their lumps of flesh.
--Will that be the case solely with great priests?


I exchange Son (Zen) questions and answers
With the Jordan bird-flower.
--What is the reason I live in this world?
--Just enjoy the flowers.

## 52. Fishing Village Rites No. 12

A white paper flower wanders over every wave
A white paper bird buries its bill in the wave
The wind of what sky spreads the net,
Plucking even that lone flower on the sea?
When a few fish shatter into white scales
And your body's spines shatter at the same time
In the invisible eyes of this typhoon
Before the calm laughter of the waves
As if the fishing net I cast fill the whole vacant sky
As if the vacant sky before me fills the whole fishing net.

## 53. Fishing Village Rites No. 2

A few pieces of gold, diamond and stone
That wander in the vacant sky.
Ah!
They recede far away the longer I watch,
But the sounds of the wings as they run away
Don't disappear over my head.
A few honey-bees that bumble
A few honey-bees that rush in like an arrow
Ah!
My shadow that passes over your land
Hangs white on the ash tree on a distant hill.

## 54. Fishing Village Rites No. 3

Look at the soul floating in the vacant sky.

His field of vision where a paper crane dances gracefully.

Enraptured people all run out and

Await the wind that comes blazing

From a hill yonder thousands of leagues away.

It's the azaleas, it's the rhododendrons;

In his field of vision flower petals fly and whirl around.

Set to fire all things to burn and hold them as a torchlight.

And look at a paper crane that floats in the vacant sky,

Look at a poor dream of one period of time.

## 55. Fishing Village Rites No. 10

Smoke from your burning bones fills the air.
I see a few pieces of bone yet to be set to fire,
I'll wait till their meaning evaporates into ash.
I'll speak to the bird that perches
At the edge of my waiting, at the end of my career.
The flames that come after their flames have passed by.

## 56. Fishing Village Rites No. 18

Even for a moment when roads that disappeared appear
    again,
The scales of a few fish glitter on the cutting block, and
Death also passes by like that;
I want to share spoken words with you
About a moment's rainbow, about a moment's rock.
Bite it--my hunting dog can run,
Run to bite you.
Ah! I want to share words with you.

## 57. Transparent Art of Metamorphosis

I tattoo my mind.
Each time I look I like them--
Those days and those nights
That suddenly rush to me out of the tattoos.

The signs I concealed among tattoos--
I like my lovers of a season
Who dance in the fishing net
When I pull the guide ropes.

Holding the wine bottle like an entertaining girl
Caressing breasts, waist and buttocks
I like the lightning and thunderbolt
I usher in as a spectacle.

I like the stars that the night sky
Plucks stitch after stitch out of its own flesh.
Reciting the primer of Chinese characters beginning
"Heaven and earth, dark and yellow..."

I like also the one game I stage
With all manner of ghosts
Erasing boundaries, erasing you and me.

I also like the metamorphosis of
Living a world by borrowing any kind of body,
Shedding off karma, transmigration and human mask.

All things and phenomena divulge their shapes, and
They say it's like the mirror reflecting
All things as they are.

A life within a mirror which you can't see
Even with such a mirror--
I cross one world with a transparent art of metamorphosis.
Ha ha ha...

## 58. Eye's Art of Metamorphosis

I applied cupping treatment over that windowpane
Using my eyes all night through.
I burned moxa.
I tattooed every spot where extravasated blood
Had oozed out.
I embroidered every place I had tattooed.

Last night my body looked like a window.
I could see all the paths in my intestines;
I saw at every bend of the meandering road
Painful love and moribund yearning floating like blood-clot
    islands.
I really felt miserable.

As they make up the dead person's face,
All night through I blew my breath into the window and my
    eyes, and
Etched in cupping, moxibustion, tattoos, stitches, one after
    another.

After I was resurrected this morning, I saw
That pretty square tambour, the embroidery of pain etched
    in the window, and

The white snow that had bloomed into a flower stitch by
    stitch.
And I saw those eyes,

Those eyes that make my body into a transparent window:
I saw your eyes.

## 59. Divulging Heavenly Secret

Women have within themselves
Bags of pigments of all colors and hues
As one extracts yellow from safflower,
Violet from gromwell, ash color from ash tree,
Blue from indigo.

Also,
Women's taste of water
Differed from color to color.
The maple-tree woman I met at the end of the hibernation
    period
Had too much water; the harder I hugged her
The more I turned into water.
The oak woman I met in springtime--
The longer I hugged her, she filled
My whole breast with cool water.

Women who, like Wulin women, practice peculiar
Arts of camouflaging and flying through space--
Each night they appeared in a thousand rivers
Like the fairy Chang-ye who flew to the moon country; or
They welcomed me wherever I went,

Having become raisin trees, wild grape vines or Korean lan-
tern-flowers.

They say, when the phoenix flaps its feathers in the mind,
The cock too becomes a phoenix.

Since that time,
All things and phenomena of this world
Have become my women,
And a treasure box of all colors in my mind.

## 60. Under the Maples, Chao-chou's Book of Poems

The fallen-maple road--
You whom I met on a path remote like flames,
You, who do not disappear,
Having stuck in my eyes.

Veins-of-leaf paths in fallen maple leaves where I kiss
With your eyes and your breaths. As I amble along that alley
You, who sit loosely anywhere and drink wine
With Li Po and Tu Fu who suddenly emerge out of
Heaps of fallen leaves,
Rainbows, twilights, waterfalls, pretty stones.

Today, you too become a fallen leaf, and
Embrace the truly good sunlight, moonlight, starlight
Till breastbones clash.
And you wonder why, while alive,
You hadn't shared these joys.

While befriending you who have abandoned blood and
    flesh
I saw myself all flaming up
Among this autumn's fallen maple leaves.

I saw our love roaming

Blending with the autumn hill's celadon glow like that.

## 61. Observation Diary, Choa-chou's Book of Poems

In this world
I opened my eyes, and
I saw myself.

The smoke from my burning flesh
Intestines within the flesh
Memories that wandered through the intestines
And the mind I had hidden as a few bones.
After burning up all of them--
All of them became visible.

So I see.
Death too is concocted by delusion.
Shivering kisses
The moonlight felt as one body
The ecstatic waiting
Even the water lights of the naked waterfall--
The index box containing these glorious delusions
Is none other than my own.

In that other world, I opened my eyes again;
It was my own room.

The hell I enter and leave several times each day
The heavenly kingdom and nirvana I visit as I wish
This room is the workplace
Where they produce them.

It is my monastery, the Buddha hall, the Zen primer and the
    Taoist temple.

My library, which made this world
In that other world
And that other world in this world--

At last I rediscovered my library in the ruins.

## 62. SF-Quasar

It's my hobby making names for stars
I give them names of literary people
Like Camus and Saint-Exupery
Or names like Marx, Nietzsche and Freud
According to bio-rhythms.
I don't charge anything for the naming.
The starlight they show to me:
That acknowledgement of gratitude is enough for me.

Today I decide to give my name
To the star that twinkles so bright by my head
But I don't entertain any illusion that that star is mine;
I'm one family with them.
That star to which I gave my name
Is only my other self.

At the end of the naming ceremony
I go up to the star and look below the sky
I find one who wakes alone and watches the stars
In the garret of a cold slanting place
And I send him warm starlight
So that his breast may become bright;
I return the starlight I received in my childhood.

## 63. Wing: Ox-Herding Pictures

As my eyesight deteriorates, things I see in my eyes
Suddenly look lovely, all alike.
Walking the streets absently,
The stones my toes kick look like jade stones.
Women I seem to have seen in movies
Flicker before my eyes as if I were wearing 3-D eyeglasses.
Also, each time my eyes kiss
Those who were born just now
Such as rabbits, ducks and chicks,
My heart leaps as if I've become their father.
What is the most wonderful of all things occurs
When my two-year-old grandson Jeongju
Snuggles up to me like wind
As I open the door back home from my day's work;
When I see very young wings flapping behind his back
As he comes flying in a wink;
When I lift him up to the ceiling forgetting my poor eye-
    sight
And see the feathers scatter and whirl dazzlingly
With laughing voices bursting out.

## 64. Tree-Friend: Poetics No. 4

I go to the forest to be friends with the trees.
Carrying bottles of raw makkoli drink,
I pour a glass for the tree's roots,
Another glass for my mind's roots.

Things like a tree's fruit, and things like bird droppings
Drop with a thud on my drunken head like a practical joke.
Those lucid trembles--
Then my words for the tree-friend swaying drunken:
"I'll take your fruit, your dung."
The tree-friend wakes being pricked by
My beard that hugs and rubs cheeks with him
And he mumbles:
I'll take your blood, your piss."

The day I visit with my tree-friend
To share dung and kisses amicably
Is my birthday, and the tree's birthday as well.

## 65. Chuang-tze Poem No. 8

The winter's children who become naked, bound by the
dream's commission, are doves;
Buried in the dove's wings the sky is showered with colors
and tints.
Winter's children are mimeographed dream words and is-
lands in that sea.
The children riding on the dragon clouds
Are wakeful islands of that sea carrying remote central
Asia's winds;
They are waves sweeping the seagull's paths.
That sea's living islands when stars fall one by one and are
set to fire.
Winter's children from darkness fold after fold
Are dream words I released from among skirts of darkness
Under the lamp glittering with its own discovery.
Clashing and clashing with their elasticity pushing out sea
water,
They are clashing and clashing as foam.

## 66. Blood's House

They say ancient people spewed blood
When they spoke their true mind;
So far I've thought the remarks are a mere metaphor.

But then today I actually spewed blood.
My head caught fire, my whole body flamed;
And fire's blood squirted out of my mouth
Allowing no time to do anything.
Blood's fountain soared.
Squatting in the sea of blood
For a very brief moment
I thought the blood's fountain that came out of me was
    very beautiful.

It was a scene ecstatic like the rainbow belt
Which intimated that my wife, who had lived with me for
    40 years,
Was returning to the heavenly kingdom.
I suddenly recalled Chuang-tze, who joyfully sang
Playing on the musical instrument
In a circumstance resembling mine.

Filling my empty inside drained of all blood

With cigarette smoke,
That day I strongly urged with great effort that
I must live well even in my wife's absence.
Though old, my face doesn't know its fate;
I was gazing into my future days in the sea of blood
Which showed only sad faces like a mirror.

## 67. The Day I Found the Snail Bride

I struck a bonanza.
As our eyes met, the Milky Way's sea route opened sparkling
    with starlight.
The sweet nature where
When I took a bite it became a peach, a tomato, a dry per-
simmon.

Though she doesn't prepare a meal,
Do the laundry or make a bed;
Though she doesn't even say, Don't drink, don't smoke,
She appears anywhere in heaven and earth when I call,
Disappears when I forget.

As old man Lao-tze said,
Man was a valley originally,
Pulling them in like a male,
Accepting them like a female.

The snail bride
Who breast-feeds when someone is thirsty and
Exorcises when someone is sick--
Infinite, ineffably infinite!

Bonanza is not something else,
Cheers, a thousand cheers.

From this hill and river,
Falling leaves, flowing water,
My lovers ran away all at once.
Infinite, ineffably infinite!
I rediscovered them all.

## 68. Black Hole in the Water

Someone calls me from within the water.
Looking in, I find a monk in a black frock.
He comes out of the water and shakes off the water,
And he turns out to be Avalokitesvara.

Someone calls me from within the water.
Wondering who it may be this time, I find a jar.
It comes out of the water and drinks the water;
And it's the Heavenly Lake on Mount Baekdu.

Water always charms me:
The water's biography the water writes down,
The vowels and consonants shown by viewing stones.

I peer into the women who live in the water.
This woman has an A-cup bra one can hold in one hand;
That woman has a smooth breast like quartz.
How versatile the way they show with their art of camou-
        flage.

Between wave and wave,
In between still other stars in the water
In between strange stars and strange galactic systems

The stars' biographies shown by the strange black hole.

The Milky Way of this night unfolding on a drawing paper
Becomes a water-drop, jumps in splashing.

## 69. Clock's Art of Metamorphosis

I took off the watch I'd worn for my whole lifetime.
I threw the watch into the night sky, commanding:
"Become a star at least."

The watch that was the first thing I peered into upon wak-
    ing--
I threw away the watch handcuff that I'd never
Taken off even to sleep.

As soon as I forgot the watch
All time moved with me as the center.

I, who had volunteered to become a prisoner, became a free
    man.
Now time is my own thing.
I even discarded my self who was dreaming
Of a better handcuff, a jewel handcuff;
I discarded and discovered me.
This night I thoughtlessly listen to the words of the star-
    light
Regenerated by my memory's hour-hand and second-hand
    and
The watch-face twinkling in the sky.

Probably love is like that,
Just like that.

## 70. Ring's Hell

As I fell in love
I learned from Nietszche the solitude of the abyss.

As I fell deeper in love,
I learned from T. S. Eliot the pain of flames.

As I loved,
I became a monster in the mirror.

As I loved,
I burned up as golden flames.

My flames roam as that sky's ring.

Even if love looks for me now
I'm the ring's curse that can't escape,
Merely going round and round within the barrel in the ring's
    hell.

## 71. SF-Correspondence

When I see a jar
I recall the transparent moon jar that showed the captured
    carp.
When I see a jar
I recall the coffin jar
In which I used to sleep breathless.

Then when I suddenly think of rain,
The jar too becomes rain.
Anywhere in the stream, in the sky, or in the earth
The rains I make, all alike, create
A memory like a jar
A love like a jar
A death like a jar.

Such jars I fill with ball-point pens;
I suddenly conceive of the rain's biography or the jar's biog-
    raphy.
Rain's lifetime accepting the Buddha who has become a
    green frog.
The lifetime of a sarira jar that lets the Buddha rest in
    there--The Buddha who is now mere sariras and bones,
    having yielded flesh and affection to fire.

Then when I suddenly write "a carp," a carp leaps out.

When I write "bean paste," I draw a jar
With a cubic ballpoint pen which gives out delicious bean
paste smell.

I mumble as I float into the sky
One of my jars which contains a memory chip of my pre-
vious life.

Moon, you moon, who played with me for thousands of
years.

## 72. Je-chun Park@age 20

Today I read again the aerial photo of Bangsan-ri, Bansan-
myeon.

A face wearing a mask that barely shows the eyes--
Eyes, with icicles formed by breath from eye and nose.
Embracing the sky's snow rushing my way with hurried gait
I copy to my breast a photo of my self at age 20 in the glac-
ier
Rolling away as a snowman.

Then,
Lee Yong-ak's girl from Jeonra province whom I met in the
glacier--
In the drum-table drinking house where a snowstorm raged
We cried "Songs, come out!; if you don't, we'll charge right
in."
In the hoarse singing voice of the Jeonra girl whose tears
swelled up
While pounding the table with chopsticks
There the trees in the deep Kangwon-province mountains
Shut their mouth, having become snow trees.
I copy to my breast
The 20 years-of-age fire of regret that burns up
Even those trees.

Attaching the 20-year-old sky I met in that song at that time,
The 20-year-old trees who wore genuine skin gloves
Over their hands and water canteens over their buttocks,
   and
The frontline hill that lies there
At full length like a cow and yawns,
I transmit them to you.

## 73. With the Bird

When I see a new leaf sprouting on a tree
I think it's like a little bird.
As I watch the numbers on the second-hand
Which, like the face of a pocket watch,
The tree branches show by mingling together,
They show a posture of threatening to leave the tree and fly
  up to the skies any moment.
I too keep an eye on the clock-face of the tree.
Perhaps those numbers will hide into the textures
Of the tree as it grows up and
Finally remain as patterns of a splintered panel.
Even then they will tell you the time when someone will
Fly away like a bird.
I come to think that
The things that sprout out of the earth's roots
Like snow
Like leaves
Always dream of such flights from the very beginning.

## 74. How Dirty the Inside of Bowels

-- Yunyan's sermon from the inanimate things


How dirty the inside of bowels--

Pushing in doggedly a ball of steamed rice,

A few chopsticks of slices of broiled fish, a few stalks of
kimchi

Mixed with anger about that guy, and envy of this chap.

How wide the inside of bowels!

The fragrance of earth seeping out of every blade of grass
and

The yearning drifting in the air--

Anywhere in this world they are

Shared by things that live or don't live.

Only the dirty things among them come my way,

The way of my bowels.

## 75. Dandelion Clock

I peered into the dandelion clock.
It had no hour-hand or minute-hand,
Numberless second-hands stood there, putting together
Their heads like needle-eyes;
They were turning their ears towards the spring's hues.

At that time I was an organ, a wind.
I was putting the wind's voice over their second-hands and
    needle-eyes.

At that time, I was a palette, a paint brush.
I fed the wind's dye to each second-hand of theirs.

Carrying dotted half-notes, dotted fourth-notes, and name-
    plates,
The dandelion second-hands like a fountain soared into the
    sky
And made fountain clocks.

On the wind's music score
Life's clocks, death's clocks
And musical-notes clocks were floating buoyantly.

In that moment I was a water-drop clock, a dandelion clock.

I was a newly-sprouting leaf that had barely thrust

Its eyes out of the needle-eyes, and

The spring's tongue that was tasting the wind.

## 76. Twilight Ice Cream

As soon as I open my eyes, I eat the early dawn's ice cream.
I melt under the tongue and eat the dawn's twilight spoonful
after spoonful.
Licking the lip, licking the lips that warm up touching my lip,
I melt and adore your lips.

In the multicolored beads of ice cream
I hear numberless eyebeams twinkling in rainbow colors
Ferreting out every nook and cranny of my body.

As soon as I open my eyes
My voice licks your lips like a confession, and freezes.
The ultra-sound images of my desires and seven attach-
ments
That unfold over that sky;
Among them, those dyed red and

The grief that radiates from me
Which I feel with my whole body;
As I melt under my tongue and eat spoonful after spoonful
That early dawn twilight and the ice carved into beads,
I become a snowman spontaneously, the remaining snow
Safeguarding the desolate hill and river.

## 77. Rainbow Thief

On a day a rainbow drifted in the sky--
Stealing that rainbow,
I made several faces.

All alone
I played
Putting on one after another
Angry, sad, lonesome, joyful, ecstatic face masks.

Those many faces living within me--
I met them for the first time.

I share the rainbow faces out to river-friends, insect-friends,
Goat-friends, squirrel-friends who play all alone.

"It's not mine, I simply prefer this my face."
They throw all of the offered faces up into the sky.

I too blushing
Return the rainbow to God.

Saying, it's okay, it's all right just watching--
If, so saying, he shows it to us at times,

I'm only thankful.

Even if I don't watch because I should not,

That rainbow looks down on me;

I'm embarrassed because he's aware.

## 78. Sunlight Lottery

Do you know the sunlight lottery?
The moment my eyes meet the sun
On the new year's new morning
The sunlight lottery pours my eye's way.
Have you received the sunlight lottery
That comes into our eyes riding the rainbow bridge?

God's sunlight lottery
Melting the wall of pain filling the breast
Dispelling the anger that coagulates
In each knot of the blood vessels--
When my eyes meet
The eyes of the new year on the new morning in the new
    year
Anybody can win the lottery--
Do you know the sunlight lottery?

The things that live in this world
The whole body and mind of the things that live stained
    with grime,
The hatred and sorrow knotted and lumped--
Melting them in one breath
The new year's and the new morning's sun

Rises dazzlingly, dazzlingly.
Have you received the sunlight lottery
Given out by the beloved sun?

The new year and the new morning--
Take, to your heart's content,
The sunlight lottery
That you receive with eyes and convey with eyes.
Once you receive it
The whole mind fills up with ecstasy.
And it turns the whole world into glowing light.

## 79. Snow-Flake Harmonica

Let's play on the silvery harmonica on a day when like today
    it snows.
Dotted half-notes, dotted quarter-notes that
Jump out of the harmonica make a snowman.
Let's look at our home
Where a snowman wearing millet-stalk eyeglasses and wool
    hats runs about in the blizzard.

The harmonica I play on--
Its silver coat has peeled off,
Revealing brownish copper hues here and there.
Though at the sound of the damaged harmonica
Warm tears, warm breaths
May turn the falling snow and the snow flakes into rain.

On a day when snow falls
Let's play on the silvery harmonica
Till our lips blister.
Let's see our home in each falling snow flake.
Let's see the blessing where
The falling snow becomes a flame and
Warms the breast.

## 80. Stereogram

I still say confidently that I've seen them.

The bottom of the blue lake where water's melodies breathe,
the golden sea bream that points of sand grasp, time's
patterns and stains that uphold them;

Koguryo trees—under heaps of countless colors and inside
the strange piece of paper where dots and lines inter-
mingle—where
Fruit hangs on every branch that wide leaves and needle
leaves tightly pack;

Doling out everything like ribs, buttock flesh, tears, thin
blood vessels, they suddenly snowball into one body. In
those remote pictures the man goes hawking, a woman
goes out on an outing carrying a parasol, and I go
somewhere together with the monkeys falling from
God's tree.

I still firmly believe I saw them all.

# The Translator

**Chang-Soo Ko**'s poems, in Korean and in English, have been published in Korean and American journals. He has published more than six books of poems including *Things, Their Eyes and Ears* (2013) and one of his book of poems *What the Spider Said: Poems of Chang Soo Ko* was published in English. He also translated several books of Korean poetry including *Sending the Ship out to the Stars* and *Drawing Lines: Selected Poems of Moon Dok-su*. He was awarded the Poetry Prize, the Jung-mun Literary Award, the Modern Korean Literature Translation Award (for poetry), the Bolan International Merit Award (for poetry) in Pakistan and the Lucian Blaga International Poetry Festival Grand Prize in Romania. He won an award at the annual poetry contest held by the American Poetry Association in 1983-1984.

CPSIA information can be obtained
at www.ICGtesting.com
Printed in the USA
FFOW03n2143260117
31784FF

9 781622 460304